GHOST WORK

GHOST WORK

ROBERT COLMAN

POEMS

Palimpsest Press
1171 Eastlawn Ave.
Windsor, Ontario. N8S 3J1
www.palimpsestpress.ca

Printed and bound in Canada
Cover design and book typography by Ellie Hastings
Edited by Jim Johnstone
Cover image: Detail from "Late November" by Patricia Auvinen

Palimpsest Press would like to thank the Canada Council for the Arts
and the Ontario Arts Council for their support of our publishing
program. We also acknowledge the assistance of the Government of
Ontario through the Ontario Book Publishing Tax Credit.

LIBRARY AND ARCHIVES CANADA CATALOGUING IN PUBLICATION

TITLE: Ghost work : poems / Robert Colman.
NAMES: Colman, Robert, 1973- author.
IDENTIFIERS: Canadiana (print) 20230568785
           Canadiana (ebook) 20230568793

ISBN 9781990293627 (SOFTCOVER)
ISBN 9781990293634 (EPUB)
SUBJECTS: LCGFT: Poetry.

CLASSIFICATION: LCC PS8605.O473 G56 2024 | DDC C811/.6—DC23

CONTENTS

The Bell / 9

The Party

January Storm / 13
Invitation to the Party / 14
The Road and the Damage Done / 15
Watching the Exits / 16
When I Wake? / 17
The Memory Clinic: 1 / 18
Good Luck / 20
Baby and Silver / 21
Cornered at the Party / 22
Driving Home From the Restaurant, I Forget One Word / 23

Ghost Work

Name / 27
The Memory Clinic: 2 / 28
Possessions / 29
Asking After His Mother's Ghost / 30
In the Ribs of the Whale / 31
On the Inadequacy of the Trapped-Bird Metaphor / 32
Fossil Record / 33
Ghost Work / 34
Name / 35
To Test an Absence / 36
Nero / 37
Clearing the Snowdrift / 38

Lost on the Way to Tortosa

Soft Estate / 41
Barter and Make / 42
Lost on the Way to Tortosa / 43
Invitation to the End / 49
On Hearing Dad Sing The Skye Boat Song From Memory / 50

We'll Meet Again

We'll Meet Again / 53
Evolution as Loss / 56
What Is Left / 57
Beneath the City, Remembering / 58
Failing Upward / 59

That Last Five Minutes

The Memory Clinic: 3 / 63
Winter Rites / 65
How You Left / 66
Preparation for the Procession / 68
May You Be Free of Suffering / 69
An Unmeasured Dose / 70
That Last Five Minutes / 71
That Last Five Minutes, Again / 72
The Crowd Disperses / 73
The Blind / 74
Name / 75

To the personal support workers, hospice employees and volunteers who do what is necessary with kindness and dignity.

The Bell

I attend the Bakelite phone
in the sunroom, waiting
for your call, not expecting
the radio to carry you.
Rub the receiver, raise
the formaldehyde ghost
but it's the bell I want—
the reverberation in my fingers
collected into being.

Did I tell you? I'm gardening
from seed this year.
Trying to recall
in the way you can't now.
Memory a synonym for care,
patience, so I plant
the phone, too, its fragile,
opaque root a way
of reaching out to you.

The best hymn, likewise,
feels useless at this distance
but also belled
because it is before us,
and then our voices, our ears
and after, echo—what is
lost, the degradation Neruda
hated become umbilical,
Your voice I remember

by imagining that ringing
and then good or bad
the conversation begins
with or without you here,
I talk and talk some more
until the bell takes shape,
the copper wire lending
heat, the clapper
blooming a tenor tongue.

THE PARTY

January Storm

When I say he wandered out into the snow in his slippers
I mean there's no accounting for his movements.
He remembers nothing of panic or fear, dark houses,
ringing a doorbell to tell a neighbour he is lost.

Much like he can't account for the bruises
each time he loses his balance, each time he's mashed
like a doorbell and finds no one home,
collisions patterned into what we call a day, a week.

What do we call the lost balance of time? What gain
to argue facts with him, or repeat endlessly what's missed?
I collide with him by the year, day, week.
In that stranger's kitchen he knew his phone number, no address.

He had facts enough to repeat a code for safety. Not all amiss,
still an instinct for survival in the blackout,
but then his own kitchen a stranger's—no phone, no address,
no need to say he walked out in the snow to slip away.

Invitation to the Party

A celebration should leave a mess.
— Natalie Diaz, "That Which Cannot Be Stilled"

We request the pleasure of you
and your significance, all the "other"
that accompanies a beckoning
every room partly you now.
There'll be music and dancing,

the bar equal to our imaginations
of youth though we can't promise
that oblivion. No, the guilt
of release nudges his smile.
Come back! it asks, a wish for your story.

We are keeping him within the celebration,
we are holding, on hold,
on standby in his unclear presence.
Celebration is memory fired,
so you see the problem,

embers, the dance floor
sand in his lap, among the glasses
his jumpcut oases. He'll be pleased
to see you—this pre-made mess
wants your joy, time in his corner,

at his shoulder the hint of connection's
cleanliness. Is it foolish to want back
anticipation? The ring announcing
that first arrival? His silhouette
keeps fooling me, waiting. Otherwise

no gifts, please.

The Road and the Damage Done

"I don't recognize this road," he said,
and what weight did I give his admission?
Paused, stated it was ten years old,
streets from home. Knowledge
tars the day, remembering
no longer one thing—instead, the plot
of his dismantling on display.
I tried to blame the pace of change
but the damage was done, absence amplified.
He went quiet, stared at his hands,
and I wonder if I shouldn't have lied,
acted a stranger in this trackless suburb
that stretches out, mapless as my words.

Watching the Exits

Forty-six, watching the exits, my mouth,
but something else crouches out of sight.
The "why the fuck" of family habit.
Forty-six, watching the exits, mouthing
he loved me, loved me enough
for this profanity to be stifled
forty-six minutes of an hour, my mouth
an anger, resentment blotting my sight.

When I Wake?

The blinds are filthy
and praise is ill gotten.

I am not "of" or "with"
all games cancelled for the season

the father/son equation
now recognizably finite.

I ask a question so that
he is a question also.

He answers, stripped
of moods, suspicion.

I face the day not unselfish,
declaim the situation,

gather before the thin light,
fumble, half blind, an opening.

The Memory Clinic: 1

I was asked to burn the cane fields.
When I poured the petrol
and lit the match I could see
I'd pleased my family.

Grandpa and grandson looked on,
smiled through the smoke
meant to rub everything clean.
The barley was taken by ergot

I thought had poisoned me—
dream-woke in a southwestern Ontario
motel, the rising damp,
and unhasped a window

asking where, why? Thirsty,
forgetful. That's all, just forgetful.
Other grains rotted in their silos,
eaten by drunken rats. My eyes

are glaucous but I watched
owls hunting in the dusk,
saw signs of their wingbeats
in the snow, I heard shadows.

I forget the year, sleep off and on
through the day now, follow
the laugh track on the telly
but not dates and times, comings, goings,

while my children dig up the vineyard
behind the house trying to recreate
scenes from their childhoods for me.
I'm afraid it will become empty highway.

I pretend otherwise, sip faux wine,
imagine I'm in Bournemouth
where dad ferried us on holiday.
We sat by the water, watching

an algal bloom, amorphous mess of single
cells inhaling CO_2. I fold all the questions
asked of me into its shifting non-heart.
Answers escape me—run from me.

The sea's mouth pleases. Nothing
safe to drink and I'm in between—
a word that sits waiting for the right words
to contain it. Am I preserved?

Wholly me at this beach? And you—
whose side are you on, observing me?
The question not what shall burn next,
but how, in the fire, we must be.

Good Luck

He's right to be paranoid.

Everything's a tether
designed to keep him placid,

designed to hide
the rye, alternate exits.

We take what we can.

"Did you lock me in the car?"
he says when I fob

the driver's side. I reply
with spy-calibre evasiveness.

If he's canny, his lips are sealed.

Holds the line on wine
but we water and switch it,

stitch him up to stay with it,
with us. We need him sober,

as if this weren't already shit.

Despair comes as temper
but we hope for reprieve,

the good luck
that comes to good thieves.

Baby and Silver

Whenever he leaves the house he wants stricture, the order of a self-chosen noose. We pore over neckties to pick the perfect shade and pattern for a landmark year. So much to discard—a rampant lion, gold on loose-knit maroon; a regimental muddy brown with green stripes; an egg-yolk yellow and paisley that can't deny '89. It's like carbon dating, though simplified to first/second wife. Years where he sees only colour, utility. Others—what, flight? I find compromise. We choose a deep blue with baby and silver. When the knot is cinched he juts his chin, wriggles his neck upward, a turtle taking air. Squares his shoulders, ready to parade. We could make a rope of the rest, rappel out to some landscape he sees complete. Wasn't that their purpose? If I yelled "soldier" he'd probably stand at attention. And I'm sampling a knot. My voicebox… you know it's waiting with the word "freedom" implied. But I see he's smoothing his lapels, settling in. Happily sufficient. And I can't deny him even this.

Cornered at the Party

Amidst the icy cutlery,
the islands of bottles,
you don soft-booted
skates at the father-son
game, your turned ankles
struggling to hold
as boys dance around you.
Let the stick steady
the hour that runs fleet.

Why see this again?

Tonight you wait to be
engaged, hands like
a concussed enforcer's—
seeing, not seeing.
Guests come singly, shake
and circle your cardboard
laugh and laughter's echo.
Do you recognize them?
No matter the voices, no loss

if loss evades shame.

Driving Home From the Restaurant,
I Forget One Word

The night is bitter winter chill,
the car unfamiliar, streetlights yellowing the driver's face
as he concentrates on the road. Off-guard, my father
asks me, "Have you got far to drive tonight?"

The car is unfamiliar to him, the streetlights yellow my face,
but I don't know enough to say more than "a half-hour north"
when he asks me how far I have to drive tonight.
The darkness doesn't seem so vast from here,

I don't know it's not enough to say "a half-hour north."
I think only in shorthand connected to my face, my voice,
the darkness growing vaster,
the light a greasy shimmer.

I think only in shorthand connected to my face, my voice,
don't realize I am just a shape next to him, a driver
that he doesn't see, a greasy shimmer.
By his door he says, "I'll be alright from here,"

and I realize we take approximate shapes—
he is home and wondering why I stand
by his door as he says "I'll be alright from here."
I need a new cipher for my presence.

He is home and wondering why I'm here
so I say, "Dad, why don't I make us a cuppa,"
and he leaps on this cipher for my presence,
the winter night forgetting its chill.

GHOST
WORK

Name

I begin with "Father" to occlude any doubts
before questions come about my name,
before loss is confirmed.
"Father" my safe word against.

Before questions come about my name
I touch on place markers, his inner landscape.
These are my safe words against
the days the country lies barren.

I touch on place markers, internalize the landscape,
rush to integrate, expiate the time unmoored,
the country we accepted as barren.
I run on until I find an anchor

but still feel this an unreliable mooring.
What do all these pieces confirm?
I run on as if words could shape an anchor,
shape a father unoccluded, riven of doubt.

The Memory Clinic: 2

Today is... today
watching bluebirds through the blinds—
even when I can't see them
they see me. Smetana plays his way
down the Moldau. It's like the Bible,
all the firsts, and then sin.

There's a door—you weren't here
so I went through it. You'll find my house
and a Welsh poet—his basso
profundo makes me smile, I know
it so well, its large slightness,
familial, like a wedge of cheddar

but I'm not hungry. No, I don't recall
my address just now but here we are,
together, no matter—everything is loud,
though, isn't it? That rumble could be thunder
or my sister's birth—"our kid"
held aloft on millworkers' shoulders...

Outside our gran's house, here again
and when is Cheryl coming to get me?
I'll not stay. The river is rising
and we are each our single cells,
the intake, the uptake, the mechanisms...
So new. We can't be contained.

Possessions

1.
Where my father lives, pictures hang
on walls he doesn't believe are his.
"I don't know how those migrated here,"
staring at three maps of England.

2.
There's something in a gaze
when it isn't returned,
can't be given back,
when the walls
become phantom limbs
with no *I* on which to latch.

3.
"There, more eyes!"
Our nephew spies the shape
and we have to squint to see it,
the butcher knife's dimpling
while he runs to translate other surfaces—
notebook, birthday wrapping,
blankets, everything connected,
everything staring back.

Asking After His Mother's Ghost

Was she a young mother
eating buttered bread
so thick it was corporeal?
Was she hungry?

"What are you doing, sat there?"
She asked, angry,
saying what's gone unsaid,
which amounts to "run, fuck's sake,

move and scare away from the edge"
Blood come to spirit level—
the faster the better
hopeful firing of you, rusted cylinder.

Did she promise steamed pudding,
chocolates, did she try to bribe you?
The tone sounds impatient, urging,
but maybe you only remember what's needful.

She hid her money in biscuit tins,
stuffed bills between mattresses.
Did she tender a lid
spread with shillings?

What coin tossed from her realm
might mean instruction enough?
Here we play pennies
against angered love.

In the Ribs of the Whale

Before weeding Penguins and pulp fiction for the Sally Ann, my
sister photographs his den. So many books. Aspiration. Was there
a goal, once, beyond connection? I pick out a German primer,
Bertrand Russell's short fictions, a guide to coastal birds of the
United States. When did the world seem so knowable? My sister
covets his teak desk, but it is anchor, not answer, Churchillian
without a voicebox; outside this carapace of shelves, just some
wayward sailor, landlocked, the pewter ashtray his spirit lamp.
Selected wisdoms are now their own animal, wandering. When I
read to him from its rows he joins me in snatches of poetry, lifts
the book from my hand, turns it, caresses, cautiously riffling the
pages, recalling his own face.

"I used to own this," he says.

On The Inadequacy of the Trapped-Bird Metaphor

Give him logic if not sight
as he paces the house, front to back,
on waking confused. Listen

from the kitchen below,
give him the knowledge of clues
if not the rope to string them through.

Climb the stairs
and you'll see he does not clatter
for sunlight, only a place

to alight for food
while the bird, unappeased
cracks feathers in your chest.

Fossil Record

Let us be the whitened stones of a Savoyard castle
The ground meal ungleaned in the mill
The hair of Marie Antoinette's Austrian pigs
The lice crawling through Boswell's wig
A fireman's tarred helmet
Hard tack knocking in a tin mess kit
A gasmask's mouse-eared filth and rot
The ghost of a contrail from 1960-odd
The Avro Arrow at the bottom of a lake
Missions orbiting the earth, all that trash in space.

Ghost Work

On the periphery of the day's rain,
a concussion of jets. Absence
in a Chicago hotel room, a shade
flickers, gathers, takes light
and I want it to mean, to be.

If my father's body is still in Toronto,
must it follow all he has lost stays there too?
Is it his memory, or a ghost of mine?
November streets tremble beneath his Triumph
Herald, calling to a road north of Kingston.

I have been congratulating myself
on Saturdays in the pub, talking
with him but also tending
a safe space, cage of familiar,
gathering what's been undocumented.

Questions are counter-productive now.
Like watching the wind, I follow what disturbs.
Chase, catch, observe. I picture fireflies
failing in a chill. Children with jars, waiting,
filling the dark with more darkness

and to that darkness I add my own
willed absence. When inevitability hews to hurt
I run towards a mythical city
that allows me body upon body,
endless touch to help forget.

Watching the leaving, I want its safety,
the solidness of nothing, unbecoming,
only body, both of us, the animal embarrassment
of our functions. The shades
I keep naming protection.

Name

I say "Father" in every sentence.
It is reassurance, a qualifier
for statement and action,
maybe a new kind of love.

Is he reassured? Am I? I qualify each line,
ask questions as a means
to the what and why of love,
faux proof that staying in the room

to ask questions means the man I knew
is still there. Father, irascible, bruised, bled.
All proofs here are staid. We are a room
named father/son, a skein of connection

stilled there, an irascible shade, bruised, bled.
The call and response clumsier each visit,
playing at son, paper skinned connection.
I say "Father" like a sentence.

To Test an Absence

The rock we stand on is not heavy.
That is left to the water below,
the canal cut into the canyon
that muffles pitch, tamps down voices
to allow for the rustle of leaves.
This walk is not ruined by absence—
loss comes easy to the cedars,
birch peel and its sticky skin
that tests memory's rule, what we hope
we can trust as we walk above
on what seems like solid ground.

Nero

Even when he thinks it's just a body double
dad accepts the length of the black cat, Nero,
travelling to his lap from the armchair, side table.
Even when he thinks it's just a body double
it's also an ally, a lithe growl untroubled
by his stasis in this room, the hollow
of him, to us so often just a body double
of a man, stroking a cat, singing the fires like Nero.

Clearing the Snowdrift

Is there another conversation to be had? I don't know.
I scrape ice from the drive instead of waking him.
The shuck of blade on asphalt is its own incantation,
the shudder of impact invoking spirits. You hear?

I scrape ice from the drive instead of waking him
knowing my words will be empty words.
The shudder of impact invokes bones. You hear
how I feel I fail him, always the scrape of me and me.

I know my words will be empty words.
Maybe he will remember a thread of them but says little.
How I feel I fail him, always the scrape of me and me,
afraid to play the drum of memory, the contrapuntal faults.

Maybe he will remember a thread of me but says little,
his answers three words or less, cautious steps,
afraid to play the drum of memory, the contrapuntal faults.
It's a standoff. The sweep of the shovel is truer

than those answers, three words or less, cautious steps.
If there is another conversation to be had, I don't know yet how
to shake the standoff. The sweep of the shovel is truer,
the *shuck* of blade on asphalt its own incantation,

echoing the conversations kept. I don't know yet how
it ends or can keep on, or can keep him safe, unflustered, not scared
of the *shuck* of blade on asphalt and its incantation
steady as his fear when he asks, "Where am I?"

Shuck.

"Where am I?"

LOST
ON THE WAY
TO TORTOSA

Soft Estate

As the highway lanes multiply
the shape of its former verge
escapes us.
                    Cornfield? Copse?

The songbirds have disappeared.
In the quiet, their absence
vibrates
                    subcutaneously.

And when I say dad is better
than last visit

            (as if we're at the plaque
            face, tapering new lines
            against the disturbance)

I hear your bird-like words—
calm, unagitated, acquiescent.
Maybe beyond loss,

                    grief fuelling
                    the engine of the room.

Barter and Make

When he hears the clang of the knife sharpener's bell he bothers
the drawers for a towel to wrap the bread knife, the boning knife,
the cleaver. The body, he thinks—the division of labour makes
the body as much as separates it, the knuckle under the strain of
attention, how it kneels toward precision. He holds his bundle
carefully as the handles rub against cloth, fleshless. The bell is
busy against the sidewalk and he totters, is forks and spoons on
the pavement before arriving

at an ice cream truck. But of course! To haggle for a drumstick,
a carving knife for an Astro Pop. Do you mind? I think you'll
appreciate these, I don't use them anymore. But I love ice cream.
And he believes it's Wall's again, as he delivered tubs-full to
grocers and confectioners. We need flesh! He dreams. We need
fat. No more

excision, kind sir! And the young man understands. We keep
nothing. We preserve at a remove. His lover would adore this
Sheffield steel. And it makes sense to him, even as he knows
he shouldn't accept the transaction. We are trying to make a
destination. Give chance a chance. A scoop? He's all bone. Two.

Flesh will fall away,
the mistakes don't matter
if we keep each other safe.

Lost on the Way to Tortosa

1.
Everywhere, tiered groves of olives,
Romans mocking our pedestrian ambitions.

So much we want to learn
though suspicion and complaint mar

every path. Tonight we char wild boar,
lamb and rabbit. Fire leaps from the barranca,

aflame in tree boles. Yet here in the ash,
mockingly, new growth.

This is the flicker he misses, the nonsense spark.
I hear him, an ocean away, testing a tune.

Only two animals left in the donkey sanctuary.
They rush to greet us, braying Hossanahs.

2.
I pick at the branch trained to take the weight
of the farmer's drowsing legs. For the burro,

an iron ring. Dad requires introductions
to each room, each object he reaches to know,

endlessly. We give the lovers two years,
outside chance. Intimacy can't conquer a life lived.

You rattle the cage of our window to better see
the stars. Sleep refuses you.

Walk away from those trying to prove themselves
home. Voices that don't survive their echoes.

3.
Half a day in the city, I admit failure.
No plan to rush its heart, claim its knowledge.

I call my role "comfort" in his house.
Familiarity the only balm.

We grow tired of the tapas quickly.
What, by now, haven't we shared?

On the mountain, birds keep us from sleep.
But they live. "Kill us if you must!" I shout.

The drunken Brits are out in force tonight. Close the blind.
Church bells, forgotten, pitch outside their range.

4.
We are past the natural. The cell
is cracked. Shards. Mosaics, at best.

Even our memories—post-modern collage—
are forgotten in the décolletage.

Dance music buffets the rooftop patio.
A torch singes lavender into gin. Greed.

Smoke. Continuation? We've lost the plot
if there was one. Smile. Duck lips.

Vans collect garbage past midnight.
Maintain, a voice says. Stoic. Numb.

5.
Miró suggests that all hope is pared
down to one unsteady line.

We pile toothpicks on our plates,
black pudding, quails' eggs, hunting

for something new. I don't want to talk
about why we're here. Nothing

but death in facts. The point is to stay
still. Please, can we all just stop moving?

The pool's metallic floor shines like a beacon,
but the breeze is cool, no ships in sight.

6.
I walk hesitantly down the steps
into the garden: translations of hosta,

woodpeckers, muffled cars.
If only we had discussed what was coming,

if we had named it
but he had time. We talked, sensibly,

about what had been. If we're going
to disappear, why not define space?

So easy to forget singular days.
Blue sky. Contrails. Distraction.

Invitation To The End

Some part of you went before the white rhino,
but still you sit with laughter, desire,
the curve of a cat indelible in your lap.
Extinction, I think, will not startle us suddenly.
Maybe it will be like your mind. We'll be able
to forget most everything. Our doubt
will be nameless. We'll do as little with our fear.

On Hearing Dad Sing the Skye Boat Song From Memory

We cling to the fact
that the colony of bees in our garden
has yet to collapse.

WE'LL MEET AGAIN

We'll Meet Again

Blue birds hover over a warble of mother-
voice you, good boy, repeat and sing to,
nudging fascists eastward on your map
of Europe past their tin-capped Maginot
line. I don't know precisely what you
think, but imagine helmets waltzing
ashore, tossing rocks at a piano that peters
out too soon. You were bombed to this
soundtrack—auf Wiedersehn
to the doodlebugs. You smile,
but I remember a mild tic when the fire-
works would stop their whistling
and you wouldn't sing along
before the pop. You weren't attacked
that day, but maybe still shell shocked,
the guns of your stutter jamming
in the dark suburbs, German planes
ghosting the park. My father,
just smiling to the soundtrack of men
dying the traditional way—patriotically
in their soiled clothes and fear.
But what lasts in that head of yours?
Nightingales in a square near a bomb shelter
and half the words to reconstruct it
reedily borrowed from your lips—
I make a fort of it, as I once did
with paisley-woven lawn chairs—shoddy
engineer—and let you hide in your non-fear
because the fascists have been routed,
burned in their bunker. You have songs
for the brazier, and you meet again
with victory on the piano. I can't even play
chopsticks—the bellows of hatred

are alive and well, dad. No, I won't tell you.
So much I won't tell you to keep things easy.
It's hard to want a war but it's dirty
and sound, and what else to do? How else
to round up all the hate? Now I sound
like the racists, want the white sheet
of their fable parboiled. I just want a song
to dance to, a cheering section to keep us,
sensible like your shadow in a La-Z-Boy
chair. It hurts to say goodbye to sense.
I've heard you insist you're adrift in London,
Ontario. The bomb is a phone call
asking me to land you safe at home,
Big Smoke suburbs. I'm no navigator
but reciprocate your mayday, coordinate
the terrain of teak furniture, stereo, lamp,
circle your doubt until you tire of arguing,
return to the safety of your cats.
There are Junckers in the Bermuda Triangle
more solid than my maps for you,
always halfway there. You remember
hope and glory in the music while I think
how I left you standing in the middle
of the care home wondering what to do next,
because I couldn't get you seated
or pointed towards the television
you said you'd watch but didn't in your fog
of to-do. The ocean swallowed you.
I want a bell to tell me where, sweet Jesus,
where are you? Signal boost. Guide book
for what will charm you into words or ease
where the soundtrack skips too quickly
and I am dancing around shame.
Where is my spirit? I let the assholes have it
in my anger and helplessness. I forget

Hiroshima and Nagasaki, I forget Dresden,
see only your camaraderie of one
in this crooning safety net. There's Rosalie—
do you see her? In her tea dress and lace-up
brogues? I don't know. I have this idea
there's an ocean roar in your ears
and a film reel going back and forth
through the same era like my fantasies
already do at times, this imaginary life just static,
serenely erotic. Honestly, I might not mind
if the music played and played. Forgive
my laziness, dad. Just feels like there's no way
forward some days. It's summer but feels
like winter with teens hefting AR-15s
in the faces of protesters. No roses
for the stocks in this December of democracy.
You wouldn't believe me. The roses fall
in the snow, sucked down in the undertow
of complaisance. You're singing again,
seem to wonder where the music comes from
but don't ask and think in this background
hum that maybe I want the calm that comes
from some sound we can all understand.

        My son, my son,
        how we want to protect
        and feel undone.

Evolution as Loss

We've lost the ear to identify the bird.
We've lost the language of the hollow
to find it. We've lost the fingers of rivers
under city streets. We've lost the where
in our how.
                            Is there a when?
Dad, tell me a story. Anything. Take me
to a sound I can feel under my fingernails.

What Is Left

Ash was falling on Loveland
before the snow started.

When heaven came we thought
it would arrive in waves

of primary colours. We still
believe in opposites

but breathe the Vermont air.
Turn the wagons, the great

migration will be short,
a desultory trip.

Starvation looks different, too.
A domestic showering the street

with invective. Love growls
like a mastiff. Your favorite rain

is blood washing from the cement.
I can't say "do you remember"

again, our lists are tiresome
ghosts. We'll not discuss

fairness. Too many suburbanites
in the mall talking rights.

Beneath the City, Remembering

Settlement Exhibition, Reykjavik, Iceland

Privilege. I roll the word about the foundations,
this dig, long house in miniature,
heat precious this far north.

In the basement of the city, 780 AD on show.
Screens plant trees on the wall.

Press a button, light up a doorway,
a midden, a stable. We are good with dirt,
the pressed and cured.

          That's my face, there!

I can feel something more than recognition:
man and tool.

Shadows walk the screens, the field, forest edge.
Here, a place of worship,
here a kill.

          What is utility? What is purpose?

Even in this dark I identify the steaming breath
of cattle at morning, a diverted stream.

          All this "I," "me."

Very soon, the one forest on the island is gone.

I can't remember the whole—only the feast,
the barn raised proudly.

Failing Upward

I try not to ponder the politics
of lazing on the patio of this winery
downing a flight, charcuterie.
Besides, it's interrupted by
my brother being pissy,
reminding me of you, and what
am I supposed to do? Sometimes
the decent thing is to hide
your goddamn feelings. He bogarts
my buzz and don't I go all Old
Faithful—instead placating,
hiding the tension the way
you trained me. I buy some tropical
cider for later—hoppy, bitter,
but don't want to waste the sun
just metres from new connection.
These relations are us now. I want
to focus my hatred elsewhere,
understand laughter against
the terminal, a drawn bead on
a stranger released, this appetite
for rancor. Petty shit, insecurities,
but this isn't crying victim.
The view is vines and an apple orchard,
gnarled graft twisted, ordered,
tables set between the rows.
A bachelorette sedately smiles past,
late warmth, the reds and golds
showing. We are here. We should be solved.
We have no memory.

THAT LAST
FIVE MINUTES

The Memory Clinic: 3

I wake.

Do I wake?

Light. Blue.

The air is cool.

Am I new?

How do I approach
this room?

Is it wrong to wait?

Maybe there are rules

How to be

Blue intrudes
without news

Reason, a bruise

Without history

Am I still me? I breathe
toward a voice

"Dad, come eat"

My son?
Orpheus.

Am I Eurydice?

My body rises
but am I alive?

Do I wish to be?

Winter Rites

The snow's come again,
the incessant day.
The plows will come
but what will they take away?
We're done and done,
the shrinking world.
What day is it? I worry
for memory but memory's
no one's familiar.
Is this your winter rite?
To wake again to nothing
shaped like snow?
I'm lucky. My wife
shakes me and we don
our coats, walk to prove
difference, cuff the shape,
punch it, pretend
minutiae. Mark and re-
mark, stake the way.

How You Left

I saw your body
balter on a stair,
laid a hand
on your back,
palm in your
palm, and slow
we went—
you leaning blind
against me, and me
there to embank
that last sheer
fabric of skin.

Who's to say you
weren't already
ascending?

Nothing left
to be shriven,
no memories
to wrest, just
the lacuna
of disease,
weightless
man, guided
by hand and...

What? Pure trust?
Is this innocence?
I imagine gods
at your marrow,
aged hunger
taken, given anew,
where the meat
of you danced
up ahead impatient
of body, function,
mechanics of lack.

Your robe
loose
as feathers.

Preparation for the Procession

Refuse a shower
ask a shave,
the care worker scythes
rare stubble.

Ceremony. Retrieve
custom, straighten
as attendants come
to "make you comfortable."

You could barely stand
and though suspicious
of transference, allow
the ambulance.

Dignity so small
unconscious wish
smooth-jawed, they lift
your quietude, your tell.

May You Be Free of Suffering

"May you be free of suffering"
a poet wrote to me. "Free"
meaning able as long as can
be. Easy to lose urgency
or risk, turning that rush
into hangnail insistence.

I want everyone more present,
but we rehash arguments,
Christmases away
from family. Nothing to say.
Who can call the past back?
We are here to keep company,

wonder who we're comforting.
Is it salve for our own absence?
It's true, I don't suffer. Born lucky
but still afraid that I lack,
that I do not help those who need,
that I hide constantly.

I visit and he sleeps, the nurses
medicate, and more sleep.
And we do not suffer
and we do not argue
but do we disappear?

An Unmeasured Dose

Two days before the end
to ward off thrush
they swab your mouth
with rye and ginger.

Incoherent, you moan
and suck the sponge
before falling back to sleep.

You cease to be logistical.
Just noisy joy.
It was good to see you
one last time.

That Last Five Minutes

is ash in the trees, settling after a windstorm.

No birds assaulting worms on the lawn.

The vague nest of knitted doll

they've given to calm you lies in your lap.

No grip. Nothing so willful.

Occasional breaths out.

You again, singular. Sorry I've turned

you into so many pieces. All fear. No flies

that day, though I wonder if you hear them

over the chainsaw as it widens its jaw,

the mangled coda that follows

That Last Five Minutes, Again

But what takes longer to admit
are the minutes spent
debating breath.

Do I stroke your face?
I stroke your face.

Kiss the crown of your head?
I kiss the crown of your head.

All the people I failed at loving
appear as I sneak a try
at saying something
tentative
to death.

The Crowd Disperses

Staff stack tables as we load empties into the SUV.
A box of sandwiches, a flat of cakes.
Is that a creaking in the branches of the maple?
So many stories
and a reel-to-reel echoing
off-you-go-to-bed Robbie
off-you-go-to-bed
when I could only say no with tears
and you held a microphone up
so I could sing my nonsense song.

The Blind

Raccoons shatter glass in the dark
screeching their plots, spring
roughed out like gangland.
Feel their small fists
owning.

Do I listen better now,
without you?

                        So many days
your talk of thunder
appealing to my eyes while
elseways a holloway opened
your private wonder. Not to gods
but clogs on cobbles,
a mill past the close.

                    When are we?

The question I should have asked
to sound out boundaries
grope for the shape
of a world remade
in vague twilight.

                    Returning
the noise of gods in this reversal,
walking back the shattered words.

Name

The dead hide untranslated
in photos. Here a Teddy Boy,
houndstooth, mouth a bruise.
Did he imagine himself brutish?
Sepia card characters,
alphabet poses, all the hues
missed, filled in, loosed
from caricature failing
more and failing
more
        and failing.

Our fabrics spit dust.
Harvest oil grasps
the edges of every-
thing, grimaces
document us,
our measure,
out in the world,
together.

I wince at late
evidence—
too broad grin,
vacancy.
Not him.
I reduce
unfairly.
Just want
on repeat.
Not enough?
He is
smiling
with us.

Facts elide
in time—
our names
scurry
behind.

Acknowledgements

"The Bell" originally appeared in *The Pomegranate London* (U.K.).

"January Storm" and "Name" originally appeared in *Canadian Medical Association Journal*.

"Baby and Silver" first appeared in *The Malahat Review*.

"The Blind" first appeared in *Windsor Review*.

"Driving Home from the Restaurant, I Forget One Word" first appeared in *Vallum*.

"Ghost Work" and "What Is Left" appeared in *Grain*.

"Invitation to the End" originally appeared in *Acumen* (U.K.).

"Winter Rites" first appeared in *The Walrus*.

"Watching the Exits" featured in the essay "Every Saturday," published in *Canadian Notes & Queries*.

Thanks to the Ontario Arts Council Recommender Grants and the publishers responsible for distributing them, who encouraged me to believe in an audience for this work.

Thanks to the Canada Council for their generous support during the time that I was honing the manuscript.

Thanks to my editor Jim Johnstone for shepherding this book from its early stages years ago to what you see today. Such care and attention is what every writer dreams of. Thanks to publisher Aimée Parent Dunn and designer Ellie Hastings for creating such a beautiful look for this collection.

Gratitude to Katie Fewster-Yan and Evan Jones whose blurbs are poems in themselves.

Thanks to my family for making me confident enough to be able to share my version of a story we have shared.

And always, love to my wife Kristi for supporting me in all I do.

PHOTO: KRISTI EDAMURA CROSS

Robert Colman is a Newmarket, Ontario-based writer and editor.
He is the author of three previous collections of poems, including
Democratically Applied Machine (Palimpsest Press 2020), as well as
the chapbook *Factory* (Frog Hollow Press 2015).